W9-BXN-307

The Coyote

A Dillon Remarkable Animals Book

The Coyote

By
Mary Lou Samuelson and
Gloria G. Schlaepfer

 **DILLON PRESS**
New York

Maxwell Macmillan Canada
Toronto

Maxwell Macmillan International
New York   Oxford   Singapore   Sydney

Acknowledgments

The authors wish to thank Dr. Joel Weintraub, Professor of Zoology, California State University, Fullerton, for his assistance.

Photo Credits

Cover courtesy of Michael Frye; back cover courtesy of Jeff Henry.

B. "Moose" Peterson/Wildlife Research Photography: frontispiece, 8, 24, 27; Michael Frye: title page, 13, 33, 34, 35, 38; Kennan Ward/Photobank: 15; Mark Avery/Orange County *Register*: 16; Jeff Henry: 18; U.S. Fish and Wildlife Service: 21; Gloria G. Schlaepfer: 28; Dr. Allan A. Schoenherr: 41; Hope Ryden: 43, 46; Prof. Maurice Gray.

The following publishers have generously given permission to reprint material from copyrighted works: HarperCollins Publishers for "Hearing the Song" from *An Oregon Message* by William Stafford, copyright © 1987 by William Stafford; University of California Press for "How Coyote Made Different People" from *Nez Percé Texts (U. C. Pubs in Linguistics: Vol. 90)*, Haruo Aoki, copyright © 1979 by The Regents of the University of California; University of California Press for "How the Coyote Got His Special Power" from *Indian Legends of the Pacific Northwest*, Ella E. Clark, copyright © 1953 by The Regents of the University of California, copyright renewed 1981 by Ella E. Clark; Pantheon Books, a division of Random House, Inc., for the Caddo Indian legend in chapter three, from *American Indian Myths and Legends* by Richard Erdoes and Alfonso Ortiz, copyright © 1984 by Richard Erdoes and Alfonso Ortiz.

Book design by Carol Matsuyama

Library of Congress Cataloging-in-Publication Data

Samuelson, Mary Lou
    The coyote / by Mary Lou Samuelson and Gloria G. Schlaepfer — 1st ed.
      p. cm. — (A Dillon remarkable animals book)
    Summary: Describes the physical characteristics, habitat, life cycle, and history of the coyote, as well as its connection to Native Americans.
    ISBN 0-87518-560-6
      1. Coyotes—Juvenile literature. [1. Coyotes.] I. Samuelson, Mary Lou. II. Title. III. Series.
QL737.C22S33   1993
599.74'442—dc20   92-44739

Dillon Press   Maxwell Macmillan Canada, Inc.
Macmillan Publishing Company   1200 Eglinton Avenue East
866 Third Avenue   Suite 200
New York, NY 10022   Don Mills, Ontario M3C 3N1

Macmillan Publishing Company is part of the Maxwell Communication Group of Companies.

First edition
Printed in the United States of America
10 9 8 7 6 5 4 3 2 1

Contents

Facts about the Coyote

Scientific Name: _Canis latrans_

Description:
Height at Shoulders—Average 24 inches (60 centimeters)
Weight—Ranges from 15 to 44 pounds (7 to 20 kilograms)
Body Length Including Tail—39 to 53 inches (100 to 135 centimeters)
Color—A mixture of gray, brown, tan, and black; legs are reddish; throat and belly are white
Running Speed—As fast as 30 to 40 miles (48 to 64 kilometers) per hour
Physical Features—Long, slender legs; bushy tail; large, upright ears; amber eyes; long, pointed muzzle

Distinctive Habits: Known for its musical howl and bark; also communicates by body language and scent marking; found in family packs and as a solitary animal

Food: Primarily meat—rabbits, mice, wood rats, ground squirrels, woodchucks, pocket gophers, porcupines, ground birds, insects, carrion, game animals; also fruits and, depending on location, domestic animals and pets

Reproductive Cycle: Female and male usually mature at one year; may mate for life; female breeds once a year; gestation period 58 to 65 days; 5 to 7 pups in average litter; both parents raise the family; pups nurse for 7 to 9 weeks

Life Span: Up to 14 years, but most live from 6 to 8 years; 18 years in captivity

Range: Alaska to Costa Rica, throughout the continental United States, and much of western and central Canada

Habitat: Adapts to a wide variety of habitats: fields, meadows, grasslands, deserts, forests

Coyote Range in America

Former Range
(19ᵗʰ century)

Present Range
(19ᵗʰ and 20ᵗʰ centuries)

Ears upright, an alert coyote watches, listens, and waits. The long, narrow muzzle and amber eyes identify this wild canid.

Chapter 1

The Remarkable Coyote

Long before Columbus landed on the Bahama Islands in 1492, long before people crossed the Bering Strait from Asia to settle throughout the Americas, long before the glaciers of the ice ages covered large areas of the continent, coyotes were in America.

From a distance, they watched the woolly mammoths and the fearsome saber-toothed tigers; they watched the Native Americans hunt huge herds of buffalo; they watched as covered wagons crossed the vast plains of North America—coyotes watched, learned, and **adapted**.*

Although mammoths and saber-toothed tigers became **extinct**, coyotes continued to live in the

* Words in **bold type** are explained in the glossary at the end of this book.

deserts and plains of North and Central America. They are found on no other continent. Intelligent, resourceful, and inventive, they have adapted over millions of years to changes that occurred in the land.

Great transformations took place in the 1800s, when people crossed the Mississippi River or moved north from Mexico to settle in the West. They brought cattle, sheep, and goats. They turned the wilderness into farms, ranches, and cities.

Some people believed that coyotes were **varmints,** or pests, along with wolves, mountain lions, and many other creatures. During the last 150 years every method possible has been used to rid the land of these types of animals. They've been trapped, poisoned, and hunted. More than 20 million coyotes have been killed. Yet the coyote has increased in number and expanded its **range** throughout continental North America. Native Americans say that the coyote will be the last living thing on earth. Coyotes are survivors.

The Dog Family

The coyote is a wild member of the dog family, Canidae. Fairly tall and quite thin, this multicolored **canid** can be recognized by its amber eyes, long, narrow muzzle, large, erect ears, and bushy, black-tipped tail.

The Aztec Indians in Central America first named it *coyotl*. Later, Spanish-speaking people adapted the Aztec name. It can be pronounced ki-OH-tee, but some people say KI-yot. Yet others pronounce the name ki-YOHT. There is only one **species** of coyote, and its scientific name is *Canis latrans*. The name, which means "barking dog," refers to the distinctive sounds the animal makes.

Coyote's Song

When a pet dog barks, it makes a sharp "arf, arf" or "woof, woof" sound. A wolf has a long, mournful howl. A coyote sounds like both: "Yip, yip, aw-hooo, yip, yip, aw-hooo." The notes rise and fall and change, making up the song of the coyote—the song of the desert and the voice of the West. William Stafford's poem describes his first memory of a coyote's song.

Hearing the Song

My father said, "Listen," and that subtle song
"Coyote" came to me; we heard it together.
The river slid by, its weight
moving like oil. "It comes at night,"
he said; "some people don't like it." "It sounds
dark," I said, "like midnight, rich. . . ."
His hand pressed my shoulder:
"Just listen." That's how I first heard the song.

The lonely western song "Bury Me Not on the Lone Prairie," sung by cowboys around the campfire, describes the **prairie** as the land "where the coyotes howl, and the wind blows free." In Aztec art, in pictures of the West, and in western movies, coyotes are usually depicted with head tilted up, howling at the moon or sky.

Head tilted up, a lone coyote howls during a blizzard.

Native American Stories

From the prairies, across the Rocky Mountains all the way to California, Native Americans have long told stories with the coyote as the main character. Each tribe has its own language and legends. For some Native Americans, Coyote was a powerful spirit. It was a godlike being that gave order to the universe. The Nez Percé people of the northwest plains believed in Coyote as the Creator. Narrator Sam Watters relates in this Nez Percé story how Coyote created Native Americans:

> Long, long ago, there were no people, so Coyote decided to create human beings. He built a fire, mixed the clay, and made a mold with human features: arms, legs, and a head. He put the little figure into a hot oven. But Coyote was impatient, and he took it out while it was still white and soft. He threw it away and tried again. This time Coyote left the clay in the oven too long, and it was totally black. On the third try, Coyote took great care and watched carefully for just the right time—neither too long nor too short. Coyote was pleased. "These will be The People," he said. Indians never came from any other place. They are Coyote's creation.

In legends, Coyote has human characteristics as well. He is good or evil, generous or greedy, wise or foolish. Many of the Native American stories are humorous and entertaining, and almost all of them have a moral, or a lesson. They teach that dishonesty,

For many Native Americans, the coyote was a godlike being.

greed, and vanity do not win out. In this tale from the
Karok people in the Pacific Northwest, a vain Coyote
learns a lesson:

> In the beginning, the Spirit Chief planned to
> name all the animals early one morning. The night
> before, Coyote tried to stay awake so he would be
> first in line to get a powerful name like Grizzly Bear
> or Eagle. He propped open his eyelids with sticks,
> but, alas, he fell asleep. When he awoke in the

Native Americans still enjoy telling stories about the coyote. Here, Jim Grayfeather plays the role of Coyote in a Chumash Indian dance.

morning, Spirit Chief had already given out the strong names. Coyote had to be called Coyote. He was so sad that Spirit Chief took pity on him and gave him the special powers of cunning and cleverness.

Although this is a legend, it has some truth to it, for this animal is extremely intelligent. It has a strong sense of curiosity, an excellent memory, and the

16

ability to solve problems. Author Hope Ryden relates a story about a male coyote in Yellowstone National Park trying "to carry off a cache of dead pack rats." Repeatedly, he tried to hold all of them in his mouth, but one or two would fall out. In frustration, he dropped all the bodies to the ground and stared at them. Then he got the bright idea to eat several, before easily picking up the rest and trotting off.

A genuinely American animal, the intelligent coyote is thriving in a land that is constantly changing. More coyotes live in more places than ever before. Why has this wild dog been able to survive and expand its range? Let's take a closer look at the remarkable coyote.

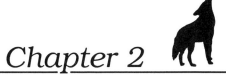

Chapter 2

A Closer Look

From a distance, you might think a coyote looks like a pet German shepherd. Both animals are about 24 inches (60 centimeters) tall at the shoulder and have similar fur color. The coyote, however, has the lean, leggy look of a long-distance runner, as its typical weight is about 22 to 25 pounds (10 to 11 kilograms). By comparison, a German shepherd is huskier and three times heavier at 60 to 85 pounds (27 to 38 kilograms). When food is plentiful, coyotes grow bigger. Larger ones, 50 pounds (23 kilograms) or more, have been found in some areas, but generally, most coyotes are medium-size canids.

Coyotes' Coats

There is a delightful Native American tale that says once upon a time coyotes were bright green; they

A coyote in Yellowstone National Park. Its thick coat of fur protects the animal against the winter's cold.

became brownish gray after rolling and tumbling in wet dirt. Although coyotes were never green, their outer coat of fur is a medley of earth colors—a little gray, tan, brown, and black. The throat and belly are white, the legs reddish. Coarse hairs on the back and neck are tipped with black.

They have two layers of fur. The grizzled outer-coat keeps them dry by shedding water, like a rain-coat. The soft undercoat of light tan fur provides warmth even in the coldest of winters.

In the late spring, when the days get longer and warmer, a change occurs in the coyote's fur. It begins to **molt**, or shed. All the thicker hairs are pushed out by a new, lighter growth. It is short, stiff and, at first, ragged looking. By the end of August, the coyote's body starts preparing for winter again. The two coats begin to thicken. Even the long, black-tipped tail grows thicker, so that in winter the coyote can curl up and wrap its bushy tail around itself, covering its nose and toes. A coyote keeps its warm fur coat until spring, and the cycle repeats.

Multicolored fur, reddish legs, and a long bushy tail characterize *Canis latrans*.

Powerful Jaws and Specialized Teeth

Coyotes are hunters of large as well as small animals. Their powerful jaws and four long, pointed **canine** teeth, or fangs, enable them to grab and hold on to their **prey**, even a wiggly jackrabbit. Their **scissor teeth** cut the meat into shreds, while the crushing **molars**, in the back of the mouth, crunch and gnaw the bones. Finally, the small, flat front **incisor** teeth clean off the last scraps of meat and gristle.

A coyote eats hungrily and quickly. It tears its food apart, swallowing large chunks without chewing. Rip, crunch, gobble, gulp—and the coyote has had a meal!

Strong Feet and Legs: Diggers and Runners

A coyote's paws have soft pads on the bottom and four toes on each foot. A fifth, undeveloped toe is also found on the front feet. Strong, blunt claws protrude from, or stick out of, the toes. The claws cannot retract, or pull back in, like a cat's claws.

The narrow front feet, or forepaws, are good diggers. A coyote will make a safe place for its pups by digging out a den deep underground. The back feet, or hind paws, are useful for scratching hard-to-reach fleas and ticks.

With their strong, muscular legs, coyotes can run for hours and jump with ease. They usually run at a trot, about 20 miles (32 kilometers) per hour, and at that gait, they travel long distances. For short spurts, 30 to 40 miles (48 to 64 kilometers) per hour is their top speed. In a full run, a coyote can easily leap 6 to 10 feet (1.8 to 3 meters) over an object.

Eyes, Ears, and Nose

Speed, endurance, and agility help a coyote in its constant search for food. These abilities, combined with good eyesight, sharp hearing, and an acute sense of smell, make the coyote a remarkable **predator**, or hunter. Native Americans say: "A feather fell from the sky. The eagle saw it, the deer heard it, the bear smelled it, and the coyote did all three." A coyote uses all three senses to survive.

A coyote's large ears act like radar antennae. The flaps, or external ears, move back and forth to catch and locate every sound. Coyotes hear faraway sounds and very faint ones that humans cannot hear, such as the tiny squeaks of mice.

Most naturalists believe coyotes can see as well as humans do. They use their eyes to detect movement or to search the sky for circling vultures—a signal that a dead animal is nearby.

It is the nose, however, that provides them with

With muscular legs and strong blunt claws, a coyote digs intensely for small prey.

the most clues to the environment. A coyote picks up the faintest **scent** because the cavity of its mouth and nose is filled with millions of cells that are sensitive to odors. Thus, coyotes follow airborne and ground scents to track prey, to communicate with other coyotes, and to avoid enemies. Most coyotes are very wary when they detect the scent of humans, for good reason.

Communication

Coyotes are social animals. They communicate with one another by smell, **vocalization,** and body language. Coyotes use urine to mark the bushes and tree trunks at the boundaries of their hunting **territories.** These are called scent posts. Other coyotes passing by leave their mark at the same spot, just as a pet dog stops at almost every tree. Coyotes are exchanging information. They are learning what other coyotes are in the area and whether they are male or female. They're finding out where a wandering pup might be or what adult female is ready to mate.

When separated by longer distances, coyotes communicate by howling. They are "talking" to one another. They might be announcing their location, warning of danger, calling to the family, predicting a storm, or just celebrating life as a wild dog. Whatever the reason, these Song Dogs are remarkable vocalists.

In face-to-face meetings, coyotes convey their moods through their expressive faces and bodies. An open, relaxed mouth, upright ears, and a wagging tail depict an animal content within its family circle. In contrast, if the hairs on the neck and shoulders bristle, if the lips curl back and the fangs show, if the tail is straight and a growl is heard, chances are the coyote is defending its kill, territory, mate, or young.

An Independent Spirit

Coyotes look and act so much like domestic dogs that some people have tried to tame an orphaned or lost pup. For Dr. William Wirtz, professor of biology, acquiring Chia began a 14-year friendship.

Did Chia learn to obey? "Not really," said Dr. Wirtz with a smile. "A coyote pet is not like a dog. Being wild, she did not have the inbred desire to please us. Even though she was housebroken, we never really trained Chia. She only did the things she wanted to."

Dr. Wirtz pointed out that Chia was affectionate and loved most people, especially children and women. She could take a dislike to some men, curling her lips and snarling at them. Chia was never allowed to run free, because Dr. Wirtz didn't know if she might harm someone.

"Having Chia as a pet was a neat experience, but

Ears back, mouth open, teeth bared, and tail down, a coyote sends a warning.

I wouldn't do it again. I wouldn't even recommend it, as it takes a very special person to raise a wild animal," emphasized Dr. Wirtz. Too independent, nervous, and fearful of strangers, a coyote cannot be completely tamed.

But one has to admire this feisty wild dog with its richly colored coat of fur, beautiful bushy tail, and bright eyes. It has keen senses, powerful jaws, shearing teeth, and strong running endurance. These characteristics serve coyotes well in their natural setting whether hunting for food or avoiding enemies. And they help explain why the Song Dog has thrived for so many centuries.

A desert coyote is tawny-brown in color to blend in with its environment.

Chapter 3

Home on the Range . . . and Beyond

Ancestors of the Coyote

Canids are part of a large group of animals called **carnivores,** or meat eaters. All carnivores **evolved** from a common ancestor—a small, primitive meat eater that lived in trees more than 60 million years ago. As **millennia** passed, different carnivore families (cats, bears, weasels) evolved, and some, like the members of the dog family, became ground dwellers.

The ancestors of canids originated in North America about 40 million years ago. Most canid species spread throughout the world, crossing the Bering Strait land bridge to Asia during the ice ages. Wolves are found in Asia, Europe, and North America, foxes in all continents except Australia, jackals in Africa and Asia, and the maned wolf in South America.

The ancestor of the coyote remained in North America. Scientists now recognize 19 subspecies, or races, of *Canis latrans*. Each subspecies occupies a specific area, or range. *Canis latrans latrans* is found throughout Montana, Wyoming, Colorado, and southern Canada; *Canis latrans texensis* on the Texas plains; *Canis latrans hondurensis* in Honduras, Central America. The races vary in body size and fur color, depending on the land they inhabit. The color is a means of **camouflage**, or hiding. A desert coyote is mostly tawny brown, the color of the desert's rocks and plants. A coyote that lives in snowy Idaho may have a cream-colored fur in winter. Animals living in the mountains tend to be larger and have darker fur.

Big Appetite

"A coyote will eat anything that doesn't eat him first!" observed writer Joe Van Wormer. A Caddo Indian legend explains coyotes' constant search for food:

In the beginning of the world, people did not die and the earth became crowded. The chiefs declared people should die, be gone for a little while, and then return. Coyote objected because he thought there still would not be enough food for everyone. So Coyote decided death should be forever, and he kept the spirits of the dead from returning. This made the people sad, and the chiefs angry. Coyote ran away. And he kept running, always looking over his shoulder, afraid that the chiefs would pursue him. Ever since then, Coyote has been hungry, because no one would give him anything to eat.

Today, hungry coyotes have an extensive wildlife menu from which to choose. They prefer small animals: rabbits, mice, ground squirrels, wood rats and gophers. When these are scarce, coyotes eat insects, cactus fruits, vegetables—just about anything.

At Yellowstone National Park, coyotes were seen eating mice and gophers as their main fare, but scientists found that they had also eaten leather gloves, strings, banana peels, orange rinds, tinfoil, and shoelaces. Scientists found traces of these "foods"

On the prowl, a coyote listens intently for sounds of small animals scurrying beneath the snow.

in the coyotes' droppings, or **scat**, and in the stomach contents of some dead coyotes.

Coyotes are definitely not squeamish eaters, since they also feed on dead animals, or **carrion.** The animals might have died naturally or been wounded by hunters or killed when crossing a road.

People also say coyotes are **opportunistic.** They take advantage of every situation in order to survive. They **scavenge,** for example, in loosely covered garbage bins and steal pet food left outside people's homes. Near farms, coyotes have killed poultry, sheep, and calves.

Locating its prey, the coyote pounces.

Even so, coyotes are more beneficial than harmful. Without them and other predators, there would be an explosion in the population of mice, rats, and rabbits. The **ecosystem** of the area they inhabit would be out of balance.

Clever Hunters

A coyote usually hunts alone or with a mate during the breeding season. A patient hunter, the coyote waits, ears and nose twitching. Slowly, silently, head down, it creeps nearer to its small prey, a few steps at a time. Again it waits, motionless. It moves a little closer. Suddenly it pounces on the unsuspecting ground squirrel. If the coyote is lucky, it catches and holds the squirrel in its forepaws. Often, though, the animal escapes safely into its hole, and the coyote goes without a meal.

Two coyotes hunting together could have better luck. One digs hastily into a ground squirrel's **burrow**, while the other waits motionless near the rodent's escape hole. Either the "digger" or the "waiter" ends up with a meal.

Coyotes have also been seen hunting with another kind of carnivore, the short, stout badger. The badger, an excellent digger with powerful claws, furiously digs into a squirrel's burrow. If the frightened rodent runs out another hole, the wily coyote is there to give chase.

Coyotes hang around farms because of the abundance of small rodents. When a thresher or plow works a field, mice and gophers are flushed out, easy prey for a watching coyote.

In the winter, when small prey are scarce, coyotes

Success! The coyote makes a meal of the rodent it has skillfully caught.

will pursue deer or pronghorn antelope. Unless the larger animal is weakened by disease or starvation, however, coyotes are generally not successful in the hunt.

Natural Enemies

A healthy deer or antelope will fight back, often trampling or mortally wounding a coyote with its sharp, pointed antlers.

Coyotes have other natural enemies. In the northern part of the continent, wolves and grizzly bears prey on coyotes. Mountain lions, found throughout the West, can kill a coyote in one crushing bite. Coyotes are wary around poisonous snakes, as the venom of a rattlesnake or copperhead can be fatal. Large predatory birds such as golden eagles or great horned owls sometimes swoop down and kill a coyote with their strong **talons**. However, in their natural setting, more coyotes die from disease (distemper, heartworm, or rabies) and starvation than from attacks by other animals.

Traps, Guns, and Poisons

The greatest enemy of coyotes is humans. People set traps for them, shoot them, and poison them.

Hinged steel traps are the oldest and most common method used. The trap is buried under a thin layer of soil near a scent post frequented by coyotes. The strong scent of urine attracts a curious coyote. SNAP! The leg is caught. Death comes slowly when the trap is not checked regularly. Some coyotes chew off their own foot to get free. Three-legged coyotes are often seen.

In the **public lands** of the western states, poison is the easiest way to kill coyotes. Poison "1080" is hidden in animal **carcasses** or placed in collars around the necks of sheep. When a coyote bites into the animal, it gets a lethal dose of poison. A newer device, M-44, "a coyote getter," shoots cyanide directly into the coyote's mouth and eyes when it pulls a baited trigger. Poisoning kills not only coyotes but other animals (bobcats, eagles, foxes, badgers, and bears) as well.

Hunters shoot coyotes for sport, luring them with the call of an injured rabbit. Members of Varmint Clubs are awarded prizes for the most coyote **pelts**. In winter, coyotes are hunted from snowmobiles.

Traps, guns, and poisons have not exterminated *Canis latrans.* Instead, these tough, opportunistic, and wary wild canids have **emigrated** to safer **habitats.** They are now the most widespread medium-size predator in North and Central America. From Alaska to Costa Rica, from the East Coast to the West Coast, coyotes make their homes.

Chapter 4

The Coyote Family

Courting and Mating

Each winter, with the onset of the **breeding season**, life in the coyote's world renews itself. Coyotes can breed as young as ten months of age, but most wait until they are 21 to 22 months old.

In late January (or even as late as March in colder climates), the often solitary and scattered canids begin their search for a mate. Rival males may fight for a female's attention, but no matter who is the victor, the female chooses the partner who will be the father of her pups.

Throughout the six-week breeding season, the two adults become a loyal pair, hunting, playing, nuzzling, and licking each other's face, or resting in

A pair of courting coyotes. After the female chooses her mate, the two become a loyal couple.

a secluded spot. They are devoted to each other and may remain mated for life.

Gestation and Birth

During the nine weeks of **gestation**, the coyotes prepare several well-concealed dens for their future family. While nearby sources of food and water are vital, the coyotes take advantage of whatever the land provides. Forest coyotes might tunnel a den beneath a hollow tree. On rocky hillsides, the pair could dig out crevices hidden by sheltering boulders. Plains and desert coyotes make their underground dens near ravines or dry streambeds. Ever opportunistic, the adults may use last year's den or enlarge the deserted den of a badger or skunk.

In early April, five to seven tiny, soft, cinnamon brown pups are born in an enlarged chamber of the den. They cannot see at birth and are totally helpless. All they know is the warmth and smell of their mother's body and milk, as they squirm, wiggle, and **nurse**. When their bellies are full, the pups sleep.

A coyote emerges from its rocky den, one of several it has prepared for its family.

For the first weeks, the mother only leaves them to go to the den entrance, where food has been left by the father coyote. He never enters the den, but he faithfully provides for his family.

Family Life

As the pups grow bigger, the mother leaves the den for periods of time to hunt with her mate, entering the den mainly to nurse the pups. In two weeks, the pups' eyes are open, and they begin to explore their home. By three to four weeks, their wobbly legs take them to the den's entrance. They tumble out, blinking in the spring sunshine.

Coyotes are devoted and watchful parents. At the slightest hint of danger, they growl a warning to the pups, who scramble to safety inside the den. If an enemy discovers the den or if the den becomes infested with pesky biting fleas, the adults abandon it and move the family to one of the spare dens.

At about five weeks, the young coyotes learn to eat meat. The parents **regurgitate** some prechewed, half-digested food. The pups sniff at it, nibble on it, then eat it all. Their diet becomes more meat and less milk, and they are soon **weaned.**

As the pups grow and their appetites increase, the adults must provide more and more food. The parents eat all they can from their kills and still carry large chunks of meat in their mouths back to the den. The pups eagerly await their return, jumping up to

A pup eagerly waits for a meal of prechewed food.

lick their faces. The parents drop the meat and bring up the partly digested food to satisfy the hungry pups.

New Skills

Soon the family spends more time outside the den. The active youngsters crawl all over their patient parents. They roll about in the dirt and play games like stalk-and-pounce or chase-and-hide that teach them survival skills. Playfully they fight to determine their rank in the litter. The largest, strongest male becomes dominant. To avoid his nipping bites, the others roll over on their backs or hunch down in submission.

Each day, the pups wander and explore farther from the den. Using their **instincts**, they chase and catch butterflies and grasshoppers. Insects are now a large part of their diet. The youngsters follow and imitate the adults as they search for food. The parents find mice nests and gopher holes and train the pups to wait patiently, hidden, until the right moment to pounce. Their lives depend upon learning these skills.

This is a dangerous time for the young and inexperienced canids. While they are hunting small animals, others—badgers, eagles, or people—may be hunting them.

As summer stretches into fall, the family drifts apart. The pups who have survived are small copies of their parents. Legs, ears, and nose have lengthened. The soft brown puppy fur is replaced with the color accents of the adult coat. Skinny tails have filled out into bushy plumes.

On Their Own

At 16 weeks, the coyotes are independent. If food is scarce in their parents' territory, they will travel miles to establish a territory of their own. But if the parents' hunting area contains enough food, the youngsters stay with them to form a small family pack. Young coyotes help care for next year's litter. Members of the pack live together but may hunt separately through autumn and winter.

In the northern climates, winter's freezing temperatures and snow blizzards are particularly difficult for the young animals. Even as agile as they are, coyotes have great difficulty moving about in soft, deep snow. The young canids often starve because they cannot hunt or because food is scarce.

In mountainous areas, coyotes follow the seasonal migrations of elk and deer to lower elevations.

Young pups test their survival skills on each other.

The weakened or diseased members of the herd become easy prey for a coyote pack.

Sometimes an elk or deer herd unknowingly provides coyotes with a quick meal. When snow covers the ground, the hoofed animals must scrape it away to reach hidden grass. Alert coyotes run in and snatch frightened mice flushed by the noisy hooves.

Even in mild climates, heavy winter rains drive

coyotes' normal rodent prey underground. Hunger makes canids bolder. They approach towns, farms, and ranches. They raid landfills, turn over garbage cans, and devour roaming pet cats and small dogs. The carcasses of sheep and cows are a boon to the hungry coyotes.

Varmints! some say. Remarkably adaptive creatures! others reply. Encounters with these wild canids most certainly will increase as humans expand into the countryside. Will people learn to live peaceably with coyotes? Or will they continue to try to rid the land of them?

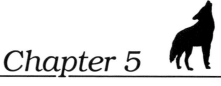

Chapter 5

Coyotes and People

Conflicting Attitudes

Native Americans have shared the coyote's world for 30,000 years. They believe that all living things are connected to one another and to the world around them. As early hunters, they accepted animal predators as a natural part of a healthy ecosystem. Indians competed equally with coyotes, wolves, and bears for food. Native Americans marveled at the coyote's patience and cunning in hunting, and respected its cleverness. The coyote was accepted for what it is, one species in a web of many.

When the Europeans arrived in North America in the 1500s, they brought with them a new way of thinking. They believed that humans should dominate the earth and control all living things. For the first 300 years or so, the newcomers remained small

To show their strong dislike of coyotes, Texas ranchers killed some of them and hung their carcasses in a tree.

in number and concentrated in the East. Land and wildlife on the continent were plentiful. Animals were killed mainly for food or fur, and predatory animals were shot if they took horses or cows.

By the mid-19th century, however, a tremendous change occurred in America, called the Westward Movement. In only 40 years, six million people settled in the Great Plains. Farms, ranches, and towns replaced the open prairies. When barbed wire fences couldn't keep wolves, grizzly bears, or mountain lions from killing livestock, the ranchers shot or poisoned the large carnivores. Thus, the coyote's big competitors were reduced in number, and it became the top predator in the food chain.

It now had new additional food sources. The "pesky varmints" found poultry and livestock just as tasty as rabbits and mice, and easier to catch. People were not happy to have coyotes for neighbors. Considered bad animals, they became targets for anyone with a gun. Many ranchers still say, "The only good coyote is a dead coyote."

From 1850 to 1885, trappers helped the ranchers by lacing the carcasses of buffalo and antelope with poison. Thousands of coyotes died. Their long-furred pelts were sold to trim the collars and cuffs of winter coats, a fashion at that time.

Government Involvement

Sheep and cattle ranchers in the late 1800s were determined to rid the land of predatory wild animals, and they asked the government for help. The campaign to exterminate coyotes began. Bounties, or rewards, were paid for each dead coyote. Since 1915, a national varmint exterminating service has been a part of the Department of Agriculture. Its methods are to shoot, poison, and trap.

In *Smithsonian* magazine, Bil Gilbert wrote, "In 1988 the feds [federal government] alone killed 76,050 coyotes. Private citizens and state and local agencies rubbed out 352,799 more of them." That year, the U.S. government spent $25 million for animal control with "coyotes a major target."

Results

Controlling does not always work as it was intended. For instance, a poorly set trap allows a coyote to escape, and it then becomes more cautious. Crippled, three-legged canids kill more livestock because they have difficulty hunting normal prey. Ranchers, in turn, demand even more control measures.

In the West, where those efforts have been extensive, that meant fewer coyotes. For those that remained, there was more food, and the survivors began to breed at an earlier age. They became more **fertile**, producing as many as 10 to 12 offspring in each litter. Nature adjusts the litter size to the food that is available.

The result of 150 years of intense control efforts is failure. Wildlife researcher Bob Crabtree has said: "The fittest [coyotes] have survived. They are harder to trap, harder to poison, harder to fence out, harder to fool, harder to kill despite all the helicopters and leg-hold traps and high-powered rifles and cyanide booby traps." The coyote population has increased, and there has been a slow but continual change in the coyotes' range. They have expanded east, north, and south into states where they had not been seen before 1900.

New Solutions

It is clear that attitudes are changing. People are beginning to see that widespread killing of predators is not an answer. They are trying other methods to protect valuable farm animals. Electric fences and guard animals are two examples.

The electrically charged wires in the fence give the predator a small jolt that scares without killing. Quick learners, few coyotes try it again.

Guard animals are used when electric fencing is impractical or too expensive. Llamas, originally from South America, have a natural aggression toward canids. They pursue and attack any coyote that approaches the sheep.

Special breeds of dogs, Anatolian or komondor, that are raised with lambs develop a strong bond with them. Later, as guard dogs, they aggressively defend the flock and drive off any predator.

Urban Coyotes

As more people move into the countryside, changing the foothills, dairy farms, and bean fields into housing developments and towns, coyotes remain. They find an urban niche wherever there is enough food and a place to hide. Brush-covered slopes and streambeds, grassy golf courses, and large wooded parks become coyotes' homes.

People are bound to encounter the animals. "A coyote grabbed my poodle!" "My beautiful cat is gone!" "Coyotes are coming into my backyard!" Angry complaints bring animal control officers to trap the "guilty" animals—a temporary solution. All a coyote wants is food; it makes no difference whether it is rabbit or cat.

In cities such as Claremont, California, where pets aren't running free and garbage is tightly covered, coyotes eat mostly rabbits, mice, and in-

Coyote Alert!

Do's and Don'ts When Living near Coyotes

Do feed pets indoors. If pets are fed out-of-doors, promptly remove food dishes when pets have finished eating.

Do clear dense weeds and brush from around your backyard.

Do put garbage in strong barrels with tight lids.

Don't put garbage or trash out the night before pick-up, but rather on the morning of the scheduled day.

Don't store bags of pet food outdoors or in the garage.

Don't feed or provide water for coyotes or other wildlife.

To Protect Children and Pets

When outside, babies, small children, and pets should be watched at all times.

Keep small dogs, rabbits, cats, and other small pets indoors. Don't allow them to run free at any time.

Fence your yard to keep out unwanted animals. Use six-foot fences with extenders and two or three strands of wire facing outward at the top. This will prevent coyotes from climbing the fence.

—Animal Control, Orange County, California

sects. Advises Dr. William Wirtz, "If you don't want coyotes in your backyard, don't provide them with anything to eat." It's a simple solution.

With their adaptability and intelligence, coyotes will survive as they have for millions of years. Perhaps it's time for people to understand and accept the role that these wild canids play in our natural environment. Coyotes are remarkably successful animals—a reminder of our special American wilderness heritage.

Sources of Information about the Coyote

Places to Contact:

Defenders of Wildlife, 1244 19th Street NW, Washington, D.C. 20036

Departments of Fish and Game in individual states

National Park Service, Office of Public Affairs, 18th & C Streets NW, Washington, D.C. 20240

Sierra Club, 730 Polk Street, San Francisco, CA 94109

United States Fish and Wildlife Service, Department of Interior, Washington, D.C. 20240

Books and Articles to Read:

Bronson, Wilfred S. *Coyotes.* New York: Harcourt, Brace & World, 1946.

Hayes, Joe. *Coyote and . . . Native American Folk Tales Retold.* Santa Fe: Mariposa Publishing, 1990.

Ryden, Hope. "The Lone Coyote Likes Family Life." *National Geographic,* August 1974.

Van Wormer, Joe. *The World of the Coyote.* A Living World Book. New York: J.B. Lippincott Co., 1974.

Glossary

adaptation (ad-ap-TAY-shun)—the ability of an animal or plant to adjust to its environment so it can survive

breeding season—the time in which animals mate and produce young

burrow (BUR-oh)—a hole in the ground made by an animal for shelter and habitation

camouflage (KAM-uh-flajh)—a disguise that is used to hide something by making it look like its surroundings

canid (KAN-id or KAY-nid)—a member of the Canidae, or dog, family, which includes wolves, foxes, and coyotes

canines (KAY-nines)—long, pointed teeth, located on each side of the top and bottom incisors, used to catch and tear meat

carcass (KAR-kuhs)—the body of a dead animal

carnivore (KAR-na-vor)—an animal that eats the flesh of other animals

carrion (KAR-ee-en)—dead and rotting flesh

ecosystem (EE-ko-sis-tem)—all living and nonliving things in a certain area or community

emigrate (EM-uh-grate)—to leave one's home and move elsewhere

evolve (ee-VOLV)—to change gradually

extinct (ik-STINKT)—no longer living anywhere on earth

fertile (FUR-til)—able to produce young

gestation (je-STAY-shun)—the time that a mother carries her young in the womb

habitat (HAB-ih-tat)—a home; the area where a plant or animal lives

incisor (in-SI-zer)—one of the front teeth between the canines

instinct (IN-stinkt)—a way of behaving that a person or animal is born with and does not have to learn

millennium (pl. **millennia**)—a period of 1,000 years

molar (MOH-ler)—one of the large teeth at the back of the mouth

molt—to shed hair, feathers, or an outer layer periodically

nurse—to take nourishment by suckling at a mother's nipple

opportunist (op-er-TOO-nist)—an animal that takes advantage of every situation for its survival

pelt—the skin of an animal

prairie (PRAR-ee)—flat or rolling land that is covered predominantly with wild grass

predator (PREHD-uh-ter)—an animal that hunts other animals for food

prey—an animal that is hunted by other animals for food

public lands—lands owned by the United States government

range—an area that an animal roams to find food

regurgitate (re-GUR-juh-tate)—to bring up incompletely digested food

scat—droppings of animals

scavenge (SKAV-enj)—to feed on carrion or trash

scent—a smell; the trail by which something can be found

scissor teeth—teeth that grow between the canines and molars. The top and bottom scissor teeth slide by each other to cut like scissors.

species (SPEE-sheez)—a group of animals or plants that have many of the same characteristics

talon (TAL-un)—the claw of a bird of prey

territory (TER-uh-tor-ee)—an area that an animal will defend against intruders of the same species

varmint (VAHR-mint)—an animal considered a pest

vocalization (vo-ka-luh-ZAY-shun)—making sound with the voice

wean—to begin to take food other than by nursing

58

Index

A graduate of Rosary College, River Forest, Illinois, Mary Lou Samuelson earned two teaching credentials at California State University, Fullerton. While teaching reading and language arts, she was a member of the California Literature Project. She is a member of the Society of Children's Book Writers. Ms. Samuelson has four grown sons and lives in California with her husband.

Gloria Schlaepfer is a community volunteer and an activist on behalf of environmental issues. Through Project Learning Tree, she shares her love of nature with schoolchildren and teachers. Her educational background includes a B.A. from Douglass College in New Jersey and an M.S. in environmental studies from California State University, Fullerton. Ms. Schlaepfer lives in Fullerton, California, with her husband and is the mother of four grown children.

60